So You  a Pet?

Written by Anne Rooney

Contents

Picking a pet   2

Dogs   4

Cats   8

Rabbits   10

Small animals   12

Fish   16

Reptiles   18

Easy pets   20

Glossary   21

Index   21

Happy pets need   22

Collins

Picking a pet

A pet makes a great friend to love, play with and look after.

Choosing a pet is exciting, but choose carefully. All animals need food, water and a suitable place to live. They and their homes must be kept clean. Large animals take up more space and cost more to keep than small animals.

Owning a pet can cost a lot in food and **vet** bills so you can only have one if your parents let you.

Some pets need exercise.

Other pets need special homes.

Dogs

Dogs come in all shapes and sizes.

Remember, puppies grow! Check how big your dog will be when it's grown up.

Dogs enjoy lots of love and attention. The more you play with your dog, the happier it will be.

All dogs need to be walked outside at least once a day. Do you have the time? A grown-up will need to take bags to pick up the dog's poo.

Large dogs need lots of exercise outside. You can't keep them in a small flat.

Dogs need **vaccinations** from the vet to keep them healthy.

Dogs need **grooming**. Most dogs enjoy having a bath.

A young dog needs **toilet training**, and **obedience training**.

You will need:

a dog bed

a collar and lead

toys

dog food

Cats

A cat looks after itself most of the time. Cats sleep a lot, so make sure your cat has a comfortable bed.

Most cats really like to be stroked, and kittens love to play.

Cats are cheaper and easier to keep than dogs. Cats clean themselves, and once they are **house-trained** they will use a **litter tray** or go outside.

As well as a cat bed, you will need:

cat food

a litter tray

Rabbits

Most rabbits live outdoors in a **hutch**. The hutch must be secure to keep the rabbit safe.

Rabbits need exercise. Put a **run** in the garden for them, or bring them indoors to run around each day.

Handle and play with your rabbit every day. Long-haired rabbits need brushing each day.

Rabbits eat dried rabbit food, hay and fresh leaves and vegetables.

As well as a hutch and food, you will need:

a brush

a water bottle

bedding

11

Small animals

Small animals such as mice, hamsters, gerbils, rats and guinea pigs are suitable if you don't have much space. Hamsters might fight if you keep them together, so it's best to have just one. But gerbils, guinea pigs, rats and mice like company. Keep two or more to keep them happy.

Some people keep **exotic** small animals, such as chinchillas, ferrets or sugar gliders.

ferret

chinchilla

sugar glider

As well as a suitable cage, you will need:

nesting material

toys

a water bottle

Choose a suitable cage so that your pet can't escape. Provide some toys to give your pet exercise and stop it getting bored.

Guinea pigs need to live outdoors in a hutch.

There is space for your pet to run around.

Your pet can hide and sleep in here.

This hutch is raised off the ground to keep unwanted animals out.

Provide soft nesting material and your pets will make their own beds.

Buy the right sort of dried food for your pet.

Clean out the cage every week.

Fish

You can keep cold-water fish or tropical fish.

Make sure you choose types of fish that can live happily together – you don't want them to eat each other! Buy the right number of fish for your tank.

cover

pump and water filter

fish tank

gravel

Clean the tank and add some fresh water each week.

Some fish like to hide in plants or tunnels.

Fish need special food.

Reptiles

Reptiles are unusual pets that need special care. Snakes, tortoises and lizards are all reptiles. They live in a heated glass tank called a vivarium that has special lighting.

a bearded agama

heat lamp

bark

pool

Tortoises can go outside in the summer if you have a safe place they can't escape from. They sleep all winter!

Tortoises eat plants, but some reptiles eat bugs or dead mice or chicks.

Easy pets

Stick insects can live in a plastic tank with a secure lid to stop them escaping.

A worm farm or ant farm is a thin, plastic tank filled with soil and sand. Add worms or ants and watch them make a home.

Sea-monkeys are tiny creatures that live in water. You buy them dried! They come with sachets of food to add to the water.

Glossary

exotic
unusual and rather fancy

grooming
brushing and washing

house-trained
uses a special place or goes outside to wee or poo

hutch
small, wooden, animal home with a sheltered sleeping area

litter tray
box of dirt or special 'litter' granules used as an animal's toilet

obedience training
training to obey commands and walk on a lead

run
a big cage for rabbits or guinea pigs to exercise outside

toilet training
training to poo and wee only outside or in a special place

vaccinations
injections to prevent an animal or person falling sick

vet
doctor for animals

water filter
electric machine for cleaning water by catching bits of dirt and plant matter

Index

ant	20
cat	8–9
chinchilla	13
dog	4–5, 7, 9
ferret	13
fish	16–17
gerbil	12
guinea pig	12, 14
hamster	12
lizard	18
mouse	12
rabbit	10–11
rat	12
sea-monkey	20
snake	18
stick insect	20
sugar glider	13
tortoise	18–19
worm	20

21

Happy pets need ...

food

 exercise

sleep

 grooming

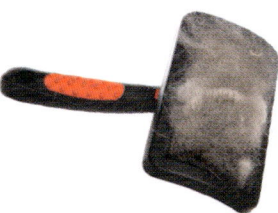

training

 playtime

23

Ideas for reading

Written by Clare Dowdall, PhD
Lecturer and Primary Literacy Consultant

Reading objectives:
- be introduced to non-fiction books that are structured in different ways
- listen to, discuss and express views about a wide range of non-fiction
- read words containing common suffixes

Spoken language objectives:
- use spoken language to develop understanding through speculating, imagining and exploring ideas
- give well-structured descriptions, explanations and narratives for different purposes
- participate actively in collaborative conversations

Curriculum links: Mathematics; Computing

Interest words: exotic, grooming, house-trained, hutch, litter tray, obedience training, run, toilet training, vaccination, vet, water filter

Word count: 650

Resources: pens and paper, squared paper, ICT

Build a context for reading

- Look at the front cover, identify each creature, and ask: Which pet would make the best pet? Why? Who has a pet?
- Read the blurb with the children. Check that children know what a sea-monkey and a stick insect is.
- Turn to the contents page. Ask children to choose which pet they would like to read about.

Understand and apply reading strategies

- Walk through the book together. Discuss the features that make this an information book, e.g. headings and subheadings, photographs with labels, information boxes, emboldened words and a glossary etc.
- Read pp 2–3 to the children. Challenge children to recount the key message, e.g. it is important to choose your pet carefully. Explain that the key message is the main information.